NDIA

y **Tim West**

Published by
Impressions Publishing
Tel: 01487 843311
www.printandpublish.co.uk

First Edition published 2011
© Tim West 2011

Printed and bound in Great Britain
Impressions Print And Publish

A catalogue record for this book
is available from The British Library
ISBN 978-1-908374-17-2

Acknowledgements

I would like to acknowledge and extend my heartfelt
gratitude to the following persons who have made this
book possible:

Andrew Grant for his vital encouragement and support
and keeping me focused, throughout this book even though
it took over our lives.

Ram Kalyan (Kelly) from Unity 101fm for his continued
support within this project.

Dipika Patel for her help and support within the Spice
section and feeding me on the way.

David Hayward without him this book would not have
published. Thank you for believing in me and pushing me
to the end.

I truly acknowledge and thank the people above for helping
me on my book

Tim West

Tim's
Quick guide to a history of Indian food

Indian cuisine is the general name for foods of the Indian subcontinent, characterized by the extensive use of various spices, herbs, and other vegetables, and sometimes fruits grown in India and also for the widespread practice of vegetarianism in Indian society. Each family of Indian cuisine includes a wide assortment of dishes and cooking techniques. As a consequence, it varies from region to region, reflecting the varied demographics of the ethnically-diverse subcontinent.

Hindu beliefs and culture have played an influential role in the evolution of Indian cuisine. However, cuisine across India also evolved as a result of the subcontinent's large-scale cultural interactions with Mongols and Britain making it a unique blend of some various cuisines. The spice trade between India and Europe is often cited as the main catalyst for Europe's Age of Discovery. The colonial period introduced European cooking styles to India, adding to the flexibility and diversity of Indian cuisine. Indian cuisine has influenced cuisines across the world, especially those from Southeast Asia and the Caribbean

"Taste a new world, on a plate"

Useful Spices & Herbs

Make easy vegetarian and meaty curries using spices

such as saffron cardamom and hot chillies

Useful Spices & Herbs

Spices commonly used in Indian cuisine.

Curry is not listed, as it is not actually a spice, but rather it is a term which refers to any Indian dish eaten with rice, or more commonly, any dish with a gravy base.

Indian spices are often heated in a pan with oil, to intensify the flavour before adding other ingredients.

Common Indian Spices	English Name	Useful Hints
Adrak	Ginger	Used as fresh and also Dried. Powder form also grated.
Aamchur/Amchoor powder	Sour Mango powder	Gives fish curries tartness.
Achar	Indian Pickle	Hundreds of varieties exist. All are interesting.
Ajmud	Celery / Radhuni seed	
Ajwain	Carom/thyme seed	
Amla	Indian gooseberry	
Anardana	Pomegranate seed	Dried not fresh. Is ground in Middle East.
Bazil / Basil	Spice powder	
Badam	Almond	
Choti Elaichi	Green cardamom	Malabar variety is native to Kerala.
Badi Elaichi	Black cardamom	Very earthy and darkly aromatic.
Chakra Phool	Star anise	Exotic, Chinese-influenced flavours.
Chironji	Charoli	A type of nut particularly used in making desserts.
Camiki	Mango extract	

Common Indian Spices	English Name	Useful Hints
Dalchini..............................	*Cinnamon*	Grown commercially in Kerala in southern India. two types, Cassia (common) and Royal.
Dhania..............................	*Coriander seed*	
Garam Masala.....................	*Spice mixture*	Blend of 8+ spices. Each family has their own secret recipe.
Gulab Jal..........................	*Rose water*	Flavours desserts. Heavily used in Middle East.
Gur................................	*Unrefined Sugar (Jaggery)*	From the sap of the sugar cane or date palm.
Haldi..............................	*Turmeric*	Source of "yellow colour" in many curries.
Hari dhaniya........................	*Coriander fresh*	Fresh green leaves. Otherwise Ci-lantro.
Harad /Hime.........................	*Terminalia chebula*	
Hari Mirch..........................	*Green Chili*	
Dhania powder/ Pisa Dhania...	*Coriander powder*	
Hing...............................	*Asafoetida*	Intensely aromatic - related to Truffle and Garlic.
Imli...............................	*Tamarind*	Provides tartness in South Indian curries.
Jaiphal...........................	*Nutmeg*	Whole nuts last forever. Powder, only a month.
Javitri............................	*Mace*	Mace is outer covering to nutmeg nut. Similar aroma.
Jeera..............................	*Cumin seed*	See Kali Jeera.
Jeera Goli.........................	*Cumin seed grounded into balls*	
Jethimadh..........................	*Licorice powder*	

Spices and Herbs

Common Indian Spices	English Name	Useful Hints
Kachra.........................	*Capers*	Otherwise known as Kabra, (in Hindi Karer).
Kadipatta....................	*Curry Tree or Sweet Neem leaf*	Cannot retain flavour when dried. Only use fresh.
Kaju..........................	*Cashewnut*	
Kala Namak / Sanchal.............	*Black salt*	Rock salt, but with very wired smell.
Kali Elaichi............................	*Black Cardamom*	Earthy, much used in North Indian curries.
Kali Mirchi............................	*Black pepper*	Largest producer is the southern Indian state of Kerala.
Kalonji.....................................	*Nigella seed*	
Kasoori Methi Dried..............	*Fenugreek leaf*	
Katira Goond..........................	*Tragacanth Gum*	A thickener and coating for desserts.
Kebab Cheeni..........................	*Allspice*	Tastes of Clove + cinnamon + nutmeg + bay leaf.
Kesar, Zaafraan.......................	*Saffron*	World's most expensive spice. Flavouring for rice.
Kesar miri miri.......................	*Saffron pulp*	Actually, saffron concentrate.
Khajur..................................	*Dates*	
Kokum..................................	*Garcinia indica*	
Khus Khus...........................	*Poppy seed*	
Kudampuli............................	*Garcinia gummi-gutta*	Used in fish preparations of Kerala.
Lahsun..................................	*Garlic*	
Lal Mirchi............................	*Red Chilli*	
Lavang..................................	*Cloves*	Andhra Pradesh, Kerala, Tamil Nadu and Karnataka are largest producers in India.

Spices and Herbs

Common Indian Spices	English Name	Useful Hints
Kali Mirch..............................	**Peppercorns**	
Methi leaves..........................	**Fenugreek leaf**	
Methi seeds...........................	**Fenugreek seed**	
Naaga Keshar........................		
Namak...................................	**Salt**	
Nimbu...................................	**Lemon / Lime**	
Pudina..................................	**Mint**	
Pyaz / Ganda.........................	**Onion**	
Panch Phoron........................		This is a Bengali spice mix that combines aniseed, cumin, fenugreek, mustard and nigella.
Pathar Ka Phool.....................	**Black Stone Flower**	
Pippali...................................	**Long pepper**	
Peeli Mirchi..........................	**Yellow Pepper**	
Rai..	**Brown Mustard Seed**	
Ratin jot................................	**Alkanet root**	
Safed Mirchi..........................	**White Pepper**	
Saji na phool.........................	**Citric acid**	
Sarson..................................	**Mustard seed**	
Sarson Tel.............................	**Mustard oil**	
Saunf/Sanchal.......................	**Fennel seed**	
Shahi Jeera...........................	**Caraway Seeds**	Smaller in size than regular.
Sirka.....................................	**Vinegar**	
Soa sag.................................		
Sonth....................................	**Dried ginger**	Mostly powdered.

Spices and Herbs

Common Indian Spices	English Name	Useful Hints
Suwa or Shopa......................... *Aniseed*		
Tej Patta................................ *Malabathrum, Bay Leaf*		Both Malabathrum and Bay Leaf are similar and called as Tej Patta in Hindi. however, they are from two different families with difference in taste.
Til..*Sesame seed*		
Shimla Mirch...........................*Capsicum*		
Kali Zeera...............................*Black Cumin*		Aroma between cumin and diesel fuel.
Tulsi....................................... *Holy Basil*		

Spices and Herbs

Chaat Masala

Chaat masala is a spice mix, used in Indian and Pakistani Cuisine. It typically consists of Amchoor (dried mango powder) cumin, Kala Namak, Coriander, dried Ginger, Salt, Black pepper, Asafoetida and Chilli powder.

Chaat Masala has both a sweet and sour taste. It is used to flavour all the popular fast foods of India and Pakistan like Bhelpuri, Golgappa, Aaloo Chaat and Dahi puri. It is something of an acquired taste, and can be added to all sorts of everyday foods and drinks or even eaten on its own.

Street vendors usually mix their own Chaat Masala, which is sprinkled on the chopped up fruit or fresh vegetables unless one specifically asks for it not to be added. Sometimes black salt with chilli powder alone is used.

In Pakistan it is often purchased in large amounts, where it is available in bulk form, before the Islamic month of Ramadan as different types of Chaat (especially Fruit Chaat) are prepared at sunset which is the time for the opening of the fast.

1000 ML

500 ML

500 ML

250 ML

ML

Helpful Measures

Cooking measurements can be tricky

heres an easy guide to help you on your way

Helpful Measures

15g = ½oz	6mm = ¼in
30g = 1oz	1cm = ½in
60g = 2oz	2cm = ¾in
90g = 3oz	2.5cm = 1in
125g = 4oz (¼lb)	5cm = 2in
155g = 5oz	6cm = 2½in
185g = 6oz	8cm = 3in
220g = 7oz	10cm = 4in
250g = 8oz (½lb)	13cm = 5in
280g = 9oz	15cm = 6in
315g = 10oz	18cm = 7in
345g = 11oz	20cm = 8in
375g = 12oz (¾lb)	23cm = 9in
410g = 13oz	25cm = 10in
440g = 14oz	28cm = 11in
470g = 15oz	30cm = 12in
500g = 16oz (1lb)	
750g = 24oz (1½lb)	
1000g (1kg) = 32oz (2lb)	

Abbreviations: Tablespoon = tbsp   Teaspoon = tsp

Helpful Measures

Continued..

3 teaspoons = 1 tablespoon

1/2 tablespoon = 1–1/2 teaspoons

2 tablespoons = 1 fluid ounce

4 tablespoons = 1/4 cup

5–1/3 tablespoons = 1/3 cup

8 tablespoons = 1/2 cup

10–2/3 tablespoons = 2/3 cup

12 tablespoons = 3/4 cup

16 tablespoons = 1 cup

6 tablespoons = 8 fluid ounces

1/8 cup = 2 tablespoons

1/4 cup = 4 tablespoons

1/4 cup = 2 fluid ounces

1/3 cup = 5 tablespoon. + 1 teaspoon

1/2 cup = 8 tablespoons

1 cup = 16 tablespoons

1 cup = 8 fluid ounces

1 cup = 1/2 pint

2 cups = 1 pint

2 pints= 1 quart

4 quarts (liquid) = 1 gallon

1 litre = approx. 4 cups or 1 quart

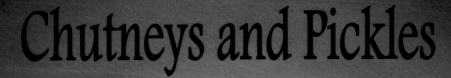

Chutneys and Pickles

There is no limit to the number of chutneys as they can be made from virtually any vegetable, fruit, herb and spice

Apple Chutney

4 Large Cloves Garlic

2 inches Ginger Root

250ml Wine Vinegar

800g Sugar

Seeds from 6 black Cardamom Pods

1/2 tsp Black Peppercorns and Cloves

500g Firm Apples (peeled and grated in long strips)

2 tsp ground red Chilli and Salt

Blend the garlic, ginger and of wine vinegar to a smooth paste in a blender or food processor. Heat the remaining wine vinegar in a heavy-based pan over a medium heat. Add the sugar and boil until the sugar has dissolved. Skim off any scum. Coarsely grind the cardamom seeds, peppercorns and cloves then add them to the pan with the remaining ingredients and bring to the boil.

Reduce the heat to medium-low and cook, uncovered, until the apple is tender and the chutney is thick. Leave to cool

Cauliflower Pickle

900g Cauliflower (cut into florets)

1 tsp Salt

1 tbsp Mustard Seeds

50g Mango Powder

1 tbsp Chilli Powder

2 tsp Ground Turmeric

1 tsp Aniseeds

6 tbsp Mustard Oil

Cook the cauliflower in boiling salted water until just tender. Drain and leave to cool. Grind together the spices and mustard oil to a paste.

Toss the cooked cauliflower in the paste and leave to marinate for 1 day in a warm place.

Store in airtight jars.

Chilli Chutney

1 Bunch Fresh Coriander

1 Bunch Fresh Mint

6–7 Green Chillies

1 tsp Chilli Powder

1/2 tsp Cumin Seeds

Pinch of Asafoetida

2 tsp Mango Powder

Salt

Juice of 1 Lemon

Grind together all the ingredients except the lemon juice, seasoning to taste with salt. Mix in the lemon juice. Serve with any main courses.

Coconut Chutney

150ml Natural Yoghurt

75g Desiccated Coconut

4 tbsp Lemon Juice

25g Fresh Coriander Leaves

15g Fresh Mint Leaves

15ml Yellow Split Peas (soak 4 hours)

1 tsp Ground Cumin

1/2 tsp Ground Red Chilli

1/2 inch ginger root (chopped)

1 Small Green Chilli

Salt (pinch)

1/2 tsp Mustard Seeds

1 tsp split Black beans (soak 4 hours)

Blend all the ingredients except the oil, asafoetida, mustard seeds and split beans in a blender or food processor to a smooth paste. Place in a bowl.

Heat the oil and fry the asafoetida and mustard seeds until the mustard seeds start crackling. Add the split beans and fry until light brown. Mix into the ground chutney and pour

Coriander Chutney

1 Bunch Fresh Coriander (coarsely chopped)
1 Medium Onion (coarsely chopped)
1 Small Green Chilli
Juice of 1 Large Lemon
1/2 tsp Ground Red Chilli
1/2 tsp Garam Masala
Salt (pinch)

Blend all the ingredients to a smooth paste in a blender or food processor then store in an airtight jar for up to 2 weeks.

Mint Chutney

100g Fresh Mint Leaves
1 Onion (chopped)
1/4 inch Root Ginger (chopped)
2 tomatoes (skinned and chopped)
4 Green Chillies (chopped)
2 tbsp Light Brown Sugar
1 tbsp Lemon Juice

Combine all the ingredients in a blender or food processor and blend to a fine paste.

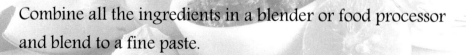

Lamb Pickle

900g Lamb (cubed)

225g Onions

1 Bulb Garlic

225g Ginger Root

450ml Mustard Oil

450ml Wine Vinegar

1 tbsp Chilli Powder

1 tbsp Mango Powder

1 tsp Cumin Seeds

6 Cardamom Pods and Cloves

1/2 tsp Grated Nutmeg

1/2 tsp Ground Mace

2 tbsp Salt

Place the meat in a heavy-based pan and cook over a low heat until the liquid from the meat dries up. Grind the onions, garlic and ginger to a paste. Heat the oil and fry the paste until browned. Add the mix and fry for 2 minutes. Add half the wine vinegar and all the remaining spices and simmer for 10 minutes, stirring continuously. Remove from the heat, stir in the remaining wine vinegar and leave to cool.

Lentil Chutney

l/2 tbsp Butter

50g Red Lentils

3 Dried Red Chillies

1/2 tsp Asafoetida

4 tbsp Grated Coconut

Salt

Heat the oil and fry the lentils, Chillies and asafoetida for 5 minutes. Add the coconut and salt to taste. Grind everything to a fine paste.

Onion Relish

3 Onions (cut into thin rings)

Juice of 2 Lemons

1 tsp Paprika

Toss all the ingredients together well, Cover and leave to marinade for 1 hour.

Chill for 1 hour before serving.

Mango Chutney

4 Large Cloves Garlic

2 inch of Ginger Root

250ml Wine Vinegar

800g Sugar

6 Black Cardamom Pods Seeds

1/2 tsp Black Peppercorns

1/2 tsp Cloves

500g firm Mango (peeled and chopped)

2 tsp Ground Red Chilli

2 tsp Salt

Blend the garlic, ginger and 3 tbsp of wine vinegar to a smooth paste in a blender or food processor. Heat the remaining wine vinegar in a heavy-based pan over a medium heat. Add the sugar and boil until the sugar has dissolved. Skim off any scum. Coarsely grind the cardamom seeds, peppercorns and cloves then add them to the pan with the remaining ingredients and bring to the boil. But don't let it burn. Reduce the heat and ad the Mango, uncovered, until the mango is tender and the chutney is thick.
Store in screw-top jars.

Sweet Mango Chutney

6 Green Mangoes
250g Cider Vinegar
225g Light Brown Sugar
6 Cloves of Garlic (sliced)
1 inch Root Ginger (thinly sliced)
1 tsp Ground Red Chilli
Salt (pinch)

Peel and slice the mangoes. Place all the ingredients in a pan and bring to the boil.

Reduce the heat and simmer gently for 30-40 minutes, stirring occasionally, until thick. Leave to cool.

Store in airtight jars.

Rice Dishes

As the world's most important crop, rice occupies a particularly rich and varied Indian cuisine

Brinjal Rice

3 Cups Plain Rice

1 1/2 tsp Mustard Seeds

A few curry leaves

3 tsp Vegetable Oil

3 Cups Eggplant (Brinjals)

3 tsp Finely Sliced Green Chillies

Salt to taste

1 tsp Turmeric Powder

3 tsp Lemon Juice

Boil rice and keep aside.

In a large pan fry the mustard seeds, curry leaves, add the eggplant and green chillies. Stir on low flame, cover and cook for 10 minutes. Add salt and turmeric powder cook for another 5 minutes. Remove from fire and add lemon juice stir well and mix with the rice.
Stir gently allowing each grain to coat.

Carrot Rice

2 Cups Rice

2 Onions

5 Carrots

2 tsp Fried Groundnuts, Oil and 2 Cloves

A Small Piece of Cinnamon; a Few Curry Leaves

1 tsp broken block of Gram and Mustard Seed

1 tsp Bengal Gram, Salt to taste

Heat the pan, with oil. Add red chillies, coriander seeds, cumin seeds and fry till it turns brown. Add grated coconuts and remove from the heat. Grind it after it cools down. Grind separately, the fried groundnuts coarsely. Cook the rice and let it cool. Put the carrots in warm water. Grate it without peeling the skin. Heat oil in a pan. Add cloves, cinnamon, mustard, broken block gram and Bengal gram. Fry them. Add curry leaves and chopped onions. Once the onion is cooked, add the grated carrots. Fry till the carrots are cooked. Add rice and fry in a low flame. Add salt and the ground masala powder. Mix it well with the rice. Finally add groundnut powder and remove from the flame. Serve hot.

Coconut Rice

400g Biryani Rice

120g Desiccated Coconut

40g Butter

25g Black Gram Dhal

25g Cashew Nut (crushed)

6 Dry Chillies

2g Curry Leaves

2.5g Asafoetida Powder

20g Coriander Leaves (shredded)

Salt to taste

Boil rice and keep aside.

Fry coconut evenly to a golden colour on a slow heat.
Heat 3 dessertspoons of butter. Fry the cashew nuts and
remove. Fry the broken pieces of dry chillies, black gram
dhal, and curry leaves well. Mix rice, coconut, nuts, 1 teaspoon of butter and salt.
Serve hot garnished with coriander leaves.

Curd Rice

1 Cup Boiled Rice

2 Cups of plain Yogurt (Curd)

2 tbsp Oil

1/4 cup Milk

Coriander Leaves (finely chopped)

1-2 Green Chillies

1 tsp Chana Daal

1 tsp Urad Daal

1 tsp Mustard Seeds

1 1/2 tsp Ginger (finely chopped)

2 tbsp Desiccated Coconut

1/2 tsp Salt

In a saucepan heat 2 tablespoonful of oil.
Add mustard seeds to the oil. When the mustard seeds start
popping add chana and urad daal. After a minute, add in
the ginger, coriander and green chillies. Sauté them for a
minute. Take the pan off the gas. Add in the rice.
Mix the salt and desiccated coconut. Just before serving,
mix all the ingredients with yogurt (curd) and milk. Curd
rice is ready to be served.

Rice Dishes

Indian Fried Rice

400g Rice
100g Ghee or butter
65g Onion
2g   Cinnamon
2g   Bay leaf
1g   Peppercorns
6g   Salt

Heat the ghee in a large saucepan and add the finely sliced
onion. Fry till golden brown, remove from the pan and keep
aside. To the hot fat, add the washed and drained rice and
the spices. Keep stirring and fry for 4–5 minutes till the rice
appears glazed. Add salt and boiling water an inch above
the rice. Boil and simmer till the water is almost absorbed
and then put into a very slow oven at 250 degree and leave
for 20–25 minutes till the rice is cooked.
Serve garnished with fried onions.
Hard-boiled eggs cut in slices may also be used as a garnish.

Garlic Rice

2 cup Cooked Rice

2 tsp crashed Garlic

2 Green Chillies (chopped)

2 tbsp Cashew Nuts

1 tbsp Almonds (chopped)

1 tsp Coriander (chopped)

2 tbsp Butter

Salt and Pepper to taste

Take a heavy pan and heat butter in it. Now add garlic and green chillies to it. Once garlic turns golden in colour, add the dry fruits and roast for half a minute.

Now add the cooked rice, sprinkle salt and pepper and mix well. Garnish the Garlic Rice with fresh coriander and serve.

Onion Rice

4 Onions

2 Cardamom (elaichi)

1 Cup Rice

1/2 tsp Chilli Powder

Salt to taste

Mustard for seasoning

Heat the pressure pan and then pour oil and season
it with mustard seeds and add onions and fry till it becomes
transparent in colour.
Then add Cardamon, Chilli powder, salt and rice with two
glass of water and keep it for boiling for fifteen minutes.
once the rice boils serve it hot

Tomato Rice

2 Large Tomatoes (made into a thick puree)

1 Cup Basmati Rice (washed and soaked for ten minutes)

1 Whole Black Cardamom

1 tsp Red Chilli powder

Salt to taste

1 tsp Garam Masala powder.

1 tbsp Butter

2 Cup Water

Heat butter in a heavy pan
Put in the whole black cardamom and then the tomato
puree. Now add the dry spices, salt. Put in the rice and mix
well. Finally add the water and cook covered till done.
Serve hot.

Plain Pilau Rice

There are two ways of cooking rice basically:

* Absorption method * Draining method

500gm Basmati Rice

4 Cloves (whole)

1 small Cinnamon Stick

1 - 2 Bay leaf leaves

1 tsp Cumin Seeds

1 tsp Salt

60g Butter

4 - 5 pods Green Cardamoms

1 litre water - approximately

1 Onion (sliced)

Method 1 - Traditional (rice fried)

In a pan melt butter or ghee, add cumin, cloves, bay leaf, cinnamon and green cardamom. When they crackle add the sliced onion and sauté until the onion is a little coloured. Add the washed and drained rice and sauté for two minutes taking care that the rice does not break.

Now add the water and salt and cook with a tight lid on top for 20 - 25 minutes on low heat, undisturbed.

Plain Pilau Rice

500gm Basmati Rice

4 – 5 Cloves (whole)

1 Cinnamon Stick

1 – 2 Bay leaf leaves

1 tsp Cumin Seeds

1 tsp Salt

60g Butter

4 – 5 pods Green Cardamoms

1 litre Water – approximately

1 Onion (sliced)

Method 2 – Easy (rice boiled)

Heat all the spices in a pot with a little butter and when they crackle add a lot of hot water. When the water comes to the boil add the washed rice and continue on the high heat. Check when the rice is almost done and then drain through a colander. Once the rice has drained sprinkle fried sliced onion on top and garnish with coriander, etc.

Note: If you want the rice to be yellow in colour add 1 tsp of turmeric to the water when cooking.

Rice Dishes

Appetizers
Sides & Snacks

Indian starter food has its own unique
place within the menu

Cucumber Salad

1 Red Onion (finely chopped)

200g Cucumbers

100g Ripe Tomatoes (finely cubed)

3 –4 tbsp Cilantro (chopped)

1 Red Chilli (very finely chopped)

1 Green Chilli (very finely chopped)

1 1/2 tbsp Lemon juice

1 tbsp Oil (I use Sunflower)

1/2 tsp Black Pepper (freshly ground)

1 1/2 tsp Chat Masala

125g Salted Peanuts (roughly chopped)

Salt (to taste)

Mix red onion, cucumber, tomatoes, cilantro, chilli, lemon juice, oil, pepper and chaat masala in a bowl and mix well. This could be done some hours in advance as the flavours will improve. Just before serving, add the chopped peanuts and taste if extra salt is necessary.

Lamb Kebab

1 lb Lamb (use boned shoulder or neck fillet)

Paste

1 tsp Cumin

1 tsp Chilli powder

1/2 tsp Lemon juice

1 1/2 tsp ground Coriander

1/2 tsp Pepper

1/2 tsp Ground Ginger

1 Clove Garlic (finely chopped)

Salt to taste

Make the paste by mixing all the ingredients together.
Cut the lamb into small cubes and cover with the paste.
Leave to marinate for several hours. Thread the lamb on
skewers and brush with oil.
Cook under a medium grill until done, turning occasionally.

Bombay Potatoes

500g Potatoes (boiled and diced)
1 medium Onion (finely chopped)
2 Cloves Garlic (crushed)
A sprig of Curry Leaves
1/2 tsp each, Cumin and Mustard seeds
1/4 tsp Turmeric powder
1/2 tsp Chilli powder
2 tbsp Oil

Heat oil in a large saucepan. Fry cumin and mustard seeds. When the seeds sputter, add curry leaves, onion and garlic. Fry until golden brown. Add all ingredients and fry for 5 to 7 minutes stirring regularly, adding little water to prevent sticking to the pan, if necessary. Serve hot

Banana Bits

4 firm Bananas

2 tbsp Lemon juice

2/3 cup Vanilla yogurt

2 cups Flaked Coconut (Toasted)

How to Cook Banana Bites

Peel bananas and cut into medium to large size bite size slices. Dip each slice in lemon juice and drain off excess.

Dip each slice in yogurt and then roll covered banana slice gently in coconut to coat.

Place in Refrigerator for up to two hours before serving.

Serve with cocktail toothpicks.

Chicken Pakoras

3 fl ounces Water

1 Onion

2 Cloves Garlic

1 teaspoon Ginger

2 Green Chillies

1 tsp Coriander, Cumin powder, Garam Masala

6 oz Chickpea Flour

1/2 tsp Bicarbonate of Soda

1/2 tsp Salt

12 oz Breast of Chicken (cut into strips)

To make the spicy batter, the dry ingredients are first added together in a mixing bowl. This includes the chickpea flour, bicarbonate of soda, cumin, garam masala, coriander, salt and chilli powder. Add a puree of onion, garlic, ginger, green chillies and coriander to the dry mixture, then stir in the water. Once the batter is prepared, dip pieces of chicken into the mixture one piece at a time and fry for 6–7 minutes until golden brown. Drain and serve with mango chutney.

Samosas

Made very easy.....

In 3 easy steps

Samosa Pastry

8 oz Plain Flour
2 tsp Salt
2 tsp Vegetable Oil
80 ml warm Water

Sieve the flour and salt into a bowl. Make a well in the centre and add the oil and some of the water.

Using your hands, draw the mixture in and combine it to make a firm dough, adding more water as necessary.

Turn out onto a floured surface and knead until smooth. Cover in cling film and set aside for 30 minutes.

Turn over for Samosa fillings ,Vegetarian and Meat

Samosas

Made very easy.....   *Step 1*

Lamb Filling

1/2 lb Minced Lamb

1 tsp Cumin seeds

2 Cardamon pods

1 Onion (finely chopped)

2 tbsp Oil

1 Clove Garlic (finely chopped)

2 tsp Grated Ginger

1 tsp Garam Masala and Curry powder

Salt and Pepper to taste

Brown the lamb mince. Pour away excess fat. Set aside. Heat the oil in a frying pan and toss the cumin and cardamom in it for 1 minute. Add the onion and cook until soft and translucent. Add the garlic and ginger and fry for another 2-3 minutes. Add the garam masala and stir well.
Continue frying for another 3 minutes.

Season with salt and pepper. Allow to cool.

Appetizers, Sides and Snacks

Samosas

Made very easy.....

Vegetarian Filling

2 Potatoes

1/2 cup Peas

2 tbsp Oil

1 tsp Cumin seeds

1/2 tsp Mustard seeds

1 Onion (finely chopped)

1 Clove Garlic (finely chopped)

1 tsp Grated Ginger

1 tbsp Garam Masala and Curry powder

2 tbsp Coriander (chopped)

Salt and Pepper to taste

Peel and boil the potatoes until just cooked, then Dice. Heat the oil in a frying pan. Add the cumin and mustard seeds and toss around for about 1 minute. Add the onion and cook until soft and translucent. Add the garlic, ginger and curry powder. Stir well and fry for 1 minute. Add the potatoes and continue to fry for another 2 minutes. Add the chopped coriander and salt and pepper to taste. Allow to cool.

Samosas

To Bring it All Together

Divide the dough into 12 pieces.
Taking each piece in turn, with your hand, roll it into a ball
Flatten it out to make a circle of 5" diameter. Cut in half.

Brush the edges with water and make a cone shape.

Place some filling inside – don't overfill – then fold over the
remaining edge and seal it by pressing gently.

Deep fry the samosas a few at a time in hot oil until golden
and crisp. Drain on kitchen towel.

Onion Bhaji

2 large Onions (finely chopped)

4 tbsp Plain Flour

1 tsp Paprika

1 tsp ground Coriander

1 tsp ground Cumin

1 tsp Turmeric

1 tsp Garlic Salt

2 tsp Milk

2 Eggs, beaten

Oil for frying

Fry the onions until slightly softened. Sieve the flour and spices into a bowl. Make a batter by adding the eggs, milk and a little water to give you a smooth but slightly runny mixture. Add the onion and stir well.

Heat some oil in a wok or deep fryer and drop in spoonfuls of the batter. Fry until crisp and golden.

Drain on kitchen towel.

Serve with a selection of chutneys.

Dhokla

350gms Gram Flour (Besan)

1 cup Curd (Stirred)

Salt to taste

1 tsp Sodium Bicarbonate, Ginger (paste), Green Chilli (paste)

1 tsp Mustard Seeds, Oil and Lemon Juice

1/2 tsp Turmeric powder

Few Curry leaves

Coriander leaves (chopped)

2-3 Green Chillies (vertically slit)

In a bowl add flour, Curd and water mix well and make a smooth batter. The batter should be of thick consistency.

Add salt and set aside for 4 hours covered with a lid. Take the ginger and green chilli paste and add to the batter. Also add turmeric powder and mix well. Keep the steamer or cooker ready on gas. Grease a baking dish, In a small bowl add bi-curb, oil and lemon juice and mix well. Add this to the batter mix and blend. Pour the batter into the greased pan and steam for 10-14 minutes. Cool and cut into big cubes. Heat little oil in a small pan and add mustard seeds and curry leaves allow to splutter. Remove and pour it over dhokla.

Chapati Bread

1 cup Whole Wheat Flour
1 cup All-purpose Flour
1 tsp Salt
2 tbsp Olive Oil
3/4 cup Hot Water or as needed

In a large bowl, stir together the whole wheat flour, all-purpose flour and salt. Use a wooden spoon to stir in the olive oil and enough water to make a soft dough that is elastic but not sticky. Knead the dough on a lightly floured surface until it is smooth. Divide into 10 parts, or less if you want bigger breads. Roll each piece into a ball. Let rest for a few minutes.

Heat a skillet over a medium heat until hot, and grease lightly. On a lightly floured surface, use a floured rolling pin to roll out the balls of dough until very thin like a tortilla. When the pan starts smoking, put a chapati on it. Cook until the underside has brown spots, about 30 seconds, then flip and cook on the other side. Continue with remaining dough.

Bombay Cashew Mix

2 tbsp Coriander seeds

2 tbsp Cumin seeds

3 tbsp Avocado or Almond oil

1 tbsp hot Paprika

1/2 tbsp freshly Ground Black Pepper

1/2 tbsp Nutmeg

1/2 tbsp Cinnamon

1 tsp Salt

4 cup raw Cashew halves

Preheat oven to 375F.

Grind spice seeds in a grinder & place in a large pan. Add oil and remaining seasonings and stir together. Pour in nuts and coat well with seasonings. Divide nuts into 2 batches and spread on a greased cookie sheet.

Bake for 20 minutes, stirring every 5 minutes, until golden.

Serve warm or at room temperature.

Cool completely before storing in an airtight container.
Will keep about 2 weeks.

Lamb Kofta Kebabs

500g Lean Minced Lamb

3 tsp Paprika

2 tsp Ground Coriander

1 Egg

2 tsp Ground Cumin

1 Clove Garlic (chopped)

1/2 Chilli (finely chopped)

Cayenne Pepper (pinch)

Salt and freshly ground Black Pepper (to taste)

Place all of the kebab ingredients together in a bowl and mix together with your hands until the meat sticks together.

With damp hands, take a handful of the kebab mixture and shape into a long sausage shape around a metal skewer.

Repeat with the remaining kebab mixture, using a new skewer each time. Place the skewers under the grill for 10–12 minutes, turning them halfway, until cooked through. Slide the kebabs off the skewers and set aside

Naan Bread

1 1/2 tsp Dried Active Yeast

1 tsp Sugar

300g Plain Flour

1/2 tsp Salt

1/2 tsp Baking Powder

1 tsp Sunflower Oil

75g Natural Yoghurt

Pre-heat oven to 200°C/180°C fan assisted / Gas mark 6.

Mix the yeast with one tablespoon of warm water and stir in the sugar. Leave in a warm place for five minutes until the yeast is covered with froth. Place flour in a separate bowl and mix in the salt and baking powder. Stir in oil, yoghurt and yeast mixture and knead to a smooth dough.

Place the dough in a large mixing bowl, cover with cling film and leave to stand until dough rises and doubles in size. On a floured surface knead the dough again before splitting into 8 equal sized balls. With a rolling pin, roll each into a long oval shape about 5mm thick. Place on a greased baking tray and put it into the hot oven. Leave to bake for approx. 10 minutes until they puff up and are soft and crumbly.

Curry Dishes

Many Indian recipes appear a little

d a u n t i n g

...use the list of ingredients

Once you have assembled the spices

marinated your ingredients

you'll find the method is simple.

Basic Curry Sauce

2 lb Cooking Onions

2 oz Green Ginger

2 oz Garlic

2 3/4 pints Water

1 tsp Salt

1 8 oz tin Tomatoes

2 tbsp Vegetable Oil

1 tsp Tomato puree

1 tsp Turmeric and Paprika

Peel and rinse the onions, ginger and garlic. Slice the onions and roughly chop the ginger and garlic. Put the chopped ginger and garlic in a blender with about 1/2 a pint of the water and blend until smooth. Take a large saucepan and put in the onions, blended garlic and ginger and the rest of the water. Add the salt and bring to the boil. Turn down the heat to very low and simmer with the lid on for 40-45 minutes.

LEAVE TO COOL

Basic Curry Sauce

Continued..

Once cooled, pour about half of the boiled onion mixture into a blender and blend until perfectly smooth. Pour the blended onion mixture into a clean pan or bowl and repeat with the other half of the boiled onions.

Wash and dry the saucepan. Reserve about 4 tablespoons of the sauce at this stage to use in cooking the meat in your chosen curry.

Pour the can of tomatoes into the rinsed blender and blend until perfectly smooth (about 2 minutes).

Into the clean saucepan, put the oil, tomato puree, turmeric and paprika. Add the blended tomatoes and bring to the boil. Turn down the heat and cook, stirring occasionally, for 10 minutes. Add the onion mixture to the saucepan and bring to the boil. Turn down the heat to a simmer.
When froth rises skim this off.

Simmer for 20-25 minutes, stirring occasionally to stop the sauce sticking to the bottom of the saucepan.

Butter Chicken

1 Small Onion (finely chopped)

1 inch Root Ginger (grated)

2 Garlic Cloves (finely chopped)

2 tbsp Butter and Lemon Juice

1 tsp Garam Masala, Chilli Powder and Ground Cumin

1 Bay leaf

2 tsp Natural Yoghurt

1 cup Single Cream

1 cup Tomato Puree

Cayenne Pepper (pinch to taste)

1lb Chicken Pieces

1 tsp Garam Masala, and Oil for frying

Heat 1 tablespoon oil and fry the onion.

When it starts to soften add the garlic and ginger and fry for another couple of minutes. Add butter, lemon juice, garam masala, chilli, cumin and bay leaf. Cook, stirring for 1 min. Add the tomato puree, cream and yoghurt. Stir well, bring to the boil and simmer gently for 10 minutes.

Lamb Saag

1lb Spinach

3 Onions (finely chopped)

2 Garlic Cloves (finely chopped)

1 inch Root Ginger (grated)

1/2 tsp Chilli Powder

1 tsp Ground Coriander and Cumin Seeds

1lb Lamb Pieces (lamb steaks not stewing lamb)

2 tbsp Tomato Puree

1 tsp Garam Masala

Coriander Leaves (finely chopped)

Salt

Oil for frying

Put spinach leaves in boiling water until just cooked, then drain and chop finely. Fry the onions until soft. Add garlic and ginger and fry for another minute. Add lamb, cumin seeds, chilli powder coriander and salt to taste. Stir well and fry until the meat is browned. Add ½ cup water, and tomato puree. Cover and simmer for about 20 minutes. Add spinach and continue to simmer until the meat is cooked
(about 10-20 minutes).
Sprinkle with garam masala and coriander before serving.

Tandoori Drumsticks

2lb Chicken Drumsticks (skinned)

Marinade 1. 1 tsp Chilli Powder, 2 tbsp Lemon Juice and pinch of Salt then set aside.

Marinade 2. One small pot Natural Yoghurt, 1 tsp Chilli Powder 1 tsp Garam Masala, 1 inch Root Ginger (grated) 1 Garlic Clove (finely chopped), 2 tbsp Lemon Juice then set aside.

The next step. Mix **marinade 1**. Make deep slashes into the chicken flesh. Rub the marinade all over the chicken and leave covered in a fridge for 30 minutes. Then make up **marinade 2** and stir all the ingredients together. Rub the marinade into the chicken pieces, making sure it gets into all the slashes. Leave, covered, in the fridge to chill for a min 8 hours. Brush the chicken pieces with melted butter and grill until cooked through. When nearly cooked, brush with butter again for a nice sheen.

Chicken Biryani

A traditional feast dish.

2lb Chicken (boneless and skinless and cubed)

1 1/2lb Basmati Rice

1/2 tsp Salt

6 Onions (finely chopped)

4 Garlic Cloves (finely chopped)

1/2 inch Root Ginger (grated)

10 Cardamoms (a mix of black and green if possible)

2 Cinnamon sticks

4 Bay Leaves

1 oz Black Peppercorns and 6 Cloves

2 tsp Salt

1/2 tsp Chilli powder

2 tbsp Natural Yoghurt

2 Large Tomatoes (chopped)

Handful Coriander Leaves (washed and chopped)

Handful Mint Leaves (washed and chopped)

1 Lime (chopped)

2 Green Chillies (cored and seeded)

3 Strands Saffron (soaked in a tbsp warm water)

Oil for frying

Turn over to finish your dish,

Chicken Biryani

Continued..

Heat some oil in a large pan. Fry the onions until soft and browner than you would usually. Remove from pan and set aside. Add more oil if necessary then add garlic, ginger, cloves, cardamoms, cinnamon, black peppers, bay leaves and fry for a minute or two.

Add chicken, salt and chilli powder and fry until chicken is browned. Add yoghurt, coriander, mint, chillies, lime and most of the onions – save some for garnish. Cook stirring frequently until chicken is almost cooked.

Meanwhile cook the rice until it is almost done. Pre-heat the oven to *180°C*, gas mark 4. Grease a large lidded dish.

When rice is almost cooked, drain it and put one third of it over the bottom of the dish. Sprinkle half the saffron on top. Spread half the chicken over the rice then add another layer of rice. Sprinkle with the remaining saffron and top with chicken. Finish it off with a layer of rice. Put the reserved onions over the top, cover and bake for 20 minutes or until the rice is fully cooked.

Indian Egg Curry

4 Eggs (hard boiled)

1 Onion

2 tbsp Tomato Puree

3 Cloves of Garlic

1/2 inch Root Ginger

1-2 Green Chillies

2 tbsp Chopped Coriander Leaves

Salt To Taste

Red Chilli Powder to taste

3/4 tsp Turmeric Powder

1/2 tsp Coriander Powder

3/4 tsp Garam Masala

2-3 tbsp Vegetable Oil

1 cup Green Peas or 250g Paneer

Remove the shell of boiled eggs & keep aside.
If using Paneer cut into cubes and fry till golden & set aside
for later use. Make a paste of onion, garlic, ginger and green
chillies in a mixer or chopper.

Turn over to finish your dish,

Indian Egg Curry

Continued..

Heat oil in a large pan and add onion-garlic paste and fry till golden brown.

Add all the spices (salt, turmeric, coriander & chilli powder) except garam masala and fry for a minute and add tomato puree. Fry till it starts leaving oil.
Add a cup of water and cook till it dry's.

Now add the fried paneer cubes or green peas (which ever using) and boiled eggs.

Add 1 cup of water and bring to boil and reduce the flame.

Simmer for 10 minutes.

Garnish egg curry with garam masala and coriander leaves and serve hot with rice.

Cabbage Carrot and Onion Curry

1/2 Small Cabbage

3 Medium Carrots

2 Large Onions

1 tbsp Oil

1/2 tsp Cumin

1/4 tsp Turmeric

1/4 tsp Mustard seeds

1/4 tsp Chilli powder

1/4 tsp Coriander

1/4 tsp Cinnamon powder

1 Salt to taste

Cut the cabbage into small pieces.

In a separate container cut carrots into thin rounds.

Peel onions and cut into small pieces. In a medium-sized pan fry the onion with butter or margarine.

When onions feel soft, add mustard seeds. 30 seconds after that add cumin powder, coriander powder, and turmeric powder. Mix the spices.

Turn over to finish your dish,

Curry Main Dishes

Cabbage Carrot and Onion Curry

Continued..

Drop carrots in pan and sauté. Put the lid on for 5 minutes.

Now add cabbage. Mix all the vegetables together.

Add cinnamon powder, salt, and chilli powder.

Put the lid on .... Wait for 5 minutes.

Turn over mixture in pan. Make sure the spices don't stick to the bottom of the pan.

Put the lid back on and leave it another 8 minutes.

If you want the curry to be softer, keep the lid on longer after cooking.

Cauliflower And Red Lentil Curry

1/2 Cup Red Lentils (rinsed)

1 Small Onion (chopped)

2 tsp Madras Curry Powder

1/2 tsp Salt

1/4 tsp Turmeric

4 Plum Tomatoes (chopped)

4 Large Cauliflower Florets

1 Jalapeno Pepper (halved, seeded and thinly sliced)

1 tbsp Vegetable Oil

1 tbsp Cumin Seeds

3 Cloves Garlic (crushed)

2 tsp Ginger (minced fresh)

1/4 tsp Cayenne Pepper

2 tbsp Lemon Juice

1 tbsp Cilantro (chopped)

1 tsp Sugar

In a large saucepan over low heat, combine lentils, onions, curry powder, salt, turmeric, and 2 cups water; bring to a simmer.

Turn over to finish your dish,

Cauliflower And Red Lentil Curry

Continued..

Cover and cook, stirring occasionally, until the lentils are soft and the sauce has thickened, about 45 minutes. Add tomatoes, cauliflower, and jalapeno peppers and simmer, covered, until the cauliflower is tender, 8 to 10 minutes longer. Remove from heat.

Heat oil in a small pan over medium-high heat. Add cumin seeds and cook for about 10 seconds. Add garlic and ginger; sauté until the garlic is lightly browned, about 1 minute. Stir in cayenne and immediately add the oil-spice mixture to the cauliflower mixture. Stir in lemon juice, cilantro, and sugar. Taste and adjust seasonings with additional salt and cayenne.

Serve over rice.

Chickpea Curry

1 cup Cooked Chickpeas

2 Large Onions

2 Dried Red Chillies

1/4 lb Ginger

3 Garlic Cloves

1/2 tsp Mustard Powder

1 tsp Cumin

1/2 tsp Turmeric

1/4 tsp Cinnamon

2 tsp Vegetable Oil

Salt, to taste

1 Tomato

Peel and cut onion. Cut ginger into small pieces, add the garlic cloves, mustard powder, and cumin and blend into a paste. Cut tomato into small pieces. Over a medium heat add oil to a pan. Sauté the condiments. When the spices become thick add cut tomato. Stir and cook for 5 minutes. Add chickpeas. Turn over contents of pan. Add 2 tablespoons of water and salt. Add cinnamon powder and turmeric powder. Stir the pan. Cook for 8 to 10 minutes.

Eggplant & Spinach Curry

1/4 cup Oil

1 tsp Black Mustard Seeds

12 Garlic Cloves (minced)

2 lb Spinach (rinsed, dried and chopped)

1 medium Eggplant (Brinijals)(cut into 1/2 inch cubes)

1 inch Root Ginger (peeled and grated)

1/4 tsp Jalapeno Chillies (minced)

1/4 tsp Turmeric Powder

1/4 tsp Paprika

1/2 tsp Ground Coriander and Cumin

2 Tomatoes (finely chopped)

Salt to taste and a small sprig of Cilantro (for garnish)

Heat the oil with half of the mustard seeds in a large pan.
Add remaining mustard seeds when the cooked seeds begin
to pop. Add the garlic and sauté until tender.
Add the spinach, a small amount at a time, stir occasionally
to keep the spinach from scorching.

Eggplant & Spinach Curry

Continued..

When the spinach wilts, add the eggplant, ginger, jalapeno chillies, turmeric, paprika, coriander, and cumin.

Sauté to blend the flavours.

Cover, and cook over medium-low heat for 15 minutes.

Add the tomatoes and season to taste with salt.

Cook, uncovered, 5 minutes longer.

Garnish with cilantro.

Mutton Curry or Beef

2 tbsp Butter

1 lb Mutton / Beef (trimmed and cubed)

1 Onion (sliced)

2 Potatoes (cut in 1 inch cubes)

1 Carrot (peeled and sliced)

1 Cauliflower Florets

1 cup Eggplant (Brinjals) (cut in 1 inch cubes)

3 Cloves Garlic (crushed)

2 Green Chillies

2 tbsp Coriander (ground)

1 tbsp Chilli Powder

1 tbsp Ground Cumin

1 tbsp Ground Ginger

1 tbsp Turmeric

1 tbsp Curry Powder (or to taste)

1 tbsp Mustard Seed

1/2 cup White Vinegar

3/4 cup Coconut Cream and Rice Flour

Heat the butter in a large pan, but not to hot

Mutton Curry or Beef

Continued..

Add onions, garlic, chillies, mustard seeds, curry powder, coriander powder, chilli powder, cumin powder, turmeric powder, and ginger. (add all the spice)

Stir constantly don't let it burn, after about 1 min lower the heat and add the mutton or beef and vegetables sauté until beef is browned.

Then add diluted coconut milk and vinegar.

Simmer on very low heat until meat is nearly tender.
When vegetables and meat are tender, add rice flour mix well with a little water. Add a little salt to taste.
Add more water if necessary while it cooks.

Simmer for 45-60 min on low heat

 Serve over hot cooked rice with plain yogurt.

Lamb and Fruit Curry

1 tbsp Peanut Oil

1/2 Onion (diced)

2 Cloves Garlic (grated)

1/2 tbsp Grated Ginger

1/2 tsp Fennel Seeds

2 tbsp Curry powder

500 gm cubed Lamb from the leg

1/2 cup plain yoghurt

1 tbsp Sultanas

1 stick of Cinnamon

1 cup Peas

2 Tomatoes (diced)

1/2 cup hot Water

1 Salt (pinch)

1 tbsp Desiccated Coconut

1 Banana sliced

Heat oil in a wide non-stick pan and fry onion, garlic and ginger for about 4 min. Add fennel seeds and curry powder and stir well.

Lamb and Fruit Curry

Continued..

Add lamb and stir for a few minutes to cook meat.
Add yoghurt, sultanas, cinnamon, peas, tomato and
hot water. Season with salt and simmer.

Cover and cook for about 2 hours or until tender, stirring
occasionally during the cooking.

Add sliced banana, stir, and cook 5 min more.

Just before serving, remove cinnamon stick and stir in
coconut.

Serving Suggestion: Serve with flat Indian bread

Madras Meat Curry

1 1/2 lb Beef Steak

2 tbsp Vegetable Oil

1 Onion (finely sliced)

4 Whole Cloves

4 Green Cardamom Pods

3 Green Chillies (seeded and finely chopped)

2 Dry Red Chillies (seeded and crushed)

1 inch Fresh Ginger Root (grated)

2 Garlic Cloves (crushed)

2 tsp Ground Coriander

2 tsp Ground Turmeric

1/4 Cup Water

1/4 Cup Tamarind Nectar, see note below

1 Salt to taste

Lettuce Leaves (for garnish)

Cut beef into cubes. Heat oil in a large pan, add beef and cook until browned all over.

Madras Meat Curry

Continued..

Remove the browned meat and set aside.
Add onion, cloves and cardamom to the pan and cook,
until onion is soft and golden brown.

Stir in chillies, gingerroot, garlic, coriander and turmeric
and cook 2 minutes.

Return beef to pan, add water and cover.

Simmer 1 hour.

Stir in tamarind nectar and salt;
Simmer another 20 to 30 minutes, until beef is tender.

Serve garnished with lettuce leaves.

South Indian Fish curry

2 lb White Fish
2 Can Coconut Milk
1 Pinch Turmeric
1/2 tsp Cumin Seeds
3 medium Onions
1/2 inch Root Ginger
6 Green Chillies
4 Large Tomatoes
1 tsp Vinegar
3 tsp Butter
1 salt (pinch) to taste

Chop onions and tomatoes.
Make a paste of the turmeric, cumin, ginger and chillies.

Clean and cut the fish into sensible pieces.

South Indian Fish curry

Continued..

Heat the butter in a large pan.

Put in the onions, tomatoes and the spice-paste.

Fry for 15 minutes.

Add the salt and one can of coconut milk.

Cook for five minutes. Put in the fish. Mix well and then put the vinegar and the last can of coconut milk.

Bring to boil and remove from heat.

Serve with rice.

The garnishing is strictly optional and to taste.

Garnish with coriander leaves, onion and tomato slices and lemon wedges.

Spicy Peanut Curry

250 gm Shelled Peanuts

1/2 cup Desiccated Coconut

2 tsp Garlic (finely chopped)

1 tbsp Ground Coriander

1/2 tsp Ground Turmeric

1/2 tsp Chilli Powder

3 tbsp Oil

2 Medium Onions (finely sliced)

1 Tomato (peeled and chopped)

1 tsp Sugar

1 tsp Salt

1 cup hot water

1/2 tsp Garam Masala

2 tbsp Coriander leaves (finely chopped)

Soak peanuts in water for 2 hours,
then boil for 20 minutes.   Drain and set aside. .

Spicy Peanut Curry

Continued..

Place coconut, garlic, ground coriander, turmeric and chilli
powder in a blender and a little water and blend
to a fine paste.
Remove contents and set aside.

Heat oil and fry onions till soft and golden.
Add tomato and the blended mixture and cook, stirring,
until it smells fragrant and the oil comes to the surface.

Add peanuts, sugar, salt and 1 cup hot water.
Bring to a boil, cover and simmer for 15 minutes or until
peanuts are cooked.
Sprinkle with garam malasa and garnish with finally
chopped coriander leaves.

Serve hot with rice.

Split Pea and Coconut Curry

1 tbsp White Rice

1 tbsp Yellow Split Peas

1/4 cup Water

2 or 3 Fresh Hot Green Chillies

1 inch piece Fresh Ginger

1 tbsp Vegetable Oil

1/4 tsp Mustard Seeds

1/2 tsp Cumin Seeds

1/8 tsp Turmeric

10 Fresh Curry Leaves (or 1 tbsp Curry Powder)

2 cup Coconut Milk

1/2 tsp Salt

1 tbsp Lemon Juice

Combine rice and split peas in a bowl and rinse in several changes of water. Add 1/4 cup water and soak for 1 hour. Blend the chillies and ginger until finely pureed.

Set aside.

Coconut Brafi

1 cup Coconut (desiccated)

3/4 cup Caster Sugar

1 cup Milk

2 tbsp Butter

1/2 tsp Ground Cardamom

Heat 1 tablespoon butter in a pan.

Add the coconut and stir fry it until it looks dry.

Add the sugar and milk. Stir well and bring to the boil.

Add the cardamom powder. Boil, stirring, until thickens.

Add the remaining ghee and stir well.

Pour the mix into a greased shallow tin.

Leave to dry and then cut into squares.

Carrot Halwa

4 cups Grated Carrot

2 cups Milk

1 cup Caster Sugar

1 tbsp Butter

1/2 cup Cashews (chopped)

1/2 cup Raisins

Place the grated carrots and milk in a heavy-based saucepan and bring to the boil. Simmer until most of the milk has disappeared. Add sugar and continue to simmer, stirring, until the mixture looks dry. Turn out into a shallow dish.

Melt the butter in a frying pan and sauté the cashews and raisins until the cashews are golden brown. Sprinkle over the top of the carrot mixture.

For extra flavour, sprinkle over a pinch of ground cardamom as well. You can puree the carrots instead of grating them if you prefer a smoother texture.

Mango Yogurt

Large carton of Natural Yogurt
4 oz Caster Sugar
8 oz Mango Pulp
1/2 tsp Ground Cardamom

Whisk the yogurt and sugar together until smooth.
Strain this mixture through a muslin cloth to allow liquid
to drain off.
Put the yogurt in a large bowl.

Strain the mango pulp through sieve.
Add the drained pulp to the yogurt with the ground
cardamom.

Cover and chill in the fridge.
Serve in individual dishes decorated with pistachio nuts.

notes:

INDEX

INDEX CONTINUED

APPETIZERS SIDES AND SNACKS

CURRY DISHES

Split Pea and Coconut Curry
Continued..

Heat oil in a large pan over medium-high heat.

Add mustard, cumin, turmeric and curry leaves.

When seeds pop, stir in split pea-ginger puree. Stir-fry for about 4 minutes.

Add coconut milk and salt.

Stir with the back of a spoon until there are no lumps.

Bring to a boil, reduce heat and simmer, uncovered, for 10 minutes.

Remove from heat and stir in lemon juice.

Curry Main Dishes

Traditional Desserts

Desserts play an integral part of Indian cuisine, with milk based desserts being a predominant feature

Sabudana Kheer (Sago pudding)

2 pts Milk
1 cup Caster Sugar
1 cup Hot Water
1 cup Sago
1 tbsp Cashew nuts
1 tbsp Raisins

Wash the sago under running water until the water runs clear. Drain thoroughly. Put the milk, into a saucepan, and bring to the boil. Add the sago and return to the boil. Simmer, stirring, until the pudding thickens and the sago is cooked.

Dissolve sugar in water.

Add to the milk and sago and continue simmering until thick. Stir in the cashew nuts and raisins.
Allow to cool slightly then serve warm.
Flavour with cardamom and saffron if liked.

Narkeler Payesh   (Rice pudding)

3/4 cup Long Grain White Rice

1 1/2 cups Water

2 tbsp Raisins

2 tbsp Almonds (finely sliced)

1 tsp Ground Cardamom

1/4 cup Caster Sugar

1 1/4 cups Unsweetened Coconut Milk

Place the rice and water in a saucepan and bring to the boil. Simmer, covered, until the water is absorbed and the rice is tender. Meanwhile dissolve the sugar in the coconut milk. When the rice is ready, add the raisins, almonds and cardamom, along with the sweet milk. Stir carefully. Simmer, uncovered, for another 10 minutes or so, until the mixture has thickened.

Allow to cool slightly then serve warm garnished with chopped pistachios. If this isn't eaten immediately,
it may become a little dry.
In that case, add some milk and reheat.

Pista Kulfi

2 pts Milk

8 tsp Sugar

1/2 tsp Cardamom Seeds (ground)

1 tbsp Pistachio Nuts (skinned and thinly sliced)

1 tbsp Ground Almonds

Using a large pan, heat the milk to boiling point.
Simmer, stirring constantly, for 40 minutes or until the milk
has reduced to less than half. Remove from the heat.
Add the sugar, ground cardamom and nuts and stir well.
Leave to cool.

Pour the mixture into small ramekin dishes and cover with
Clingfilm or foil. Freeze until set. To serve, remove the kulfi
from the dish by running a hot knife inside the edge. Tip out
onto a small plate. Serve garnished with raspberry and pistachio nuts.

Illustrations, Design and Book layout by Tim West

12:50

GROUP TRAINING TECHNIQUES